DEDICATION

This book is dedicated, first and foremost, to my Lord and Savior, Jesus Christ, who has been so faithful in my life.

Special thanks to my family, especially my precious son, Jayden, a mighty man of God by faith; and Pastor Isaac Samuel II, who activated the writing gift that God
placed within me.

I also want to acknowledge all Christian parents who want to see their children and grandchildren receive Salvation—I celebrate you, and I rejoice in advance with you.

WINNING YOUR CHILD TO CHRIST

FUNDAMENTAL STEPS TO ACHIEVE THE PROMISE OF ACTS 2:39

KEBRINA T. ROBINSON

Copyright © 2020 by Kebrina T. Robinson

All rights reserved. No part of this publication may be reproduced, distributed, or transmitted in any form or by any means, without prior written permission.

Scripture quotes taken from the Holy Bible, New Living Translation (NLT) – Copyright © 1996, 2004, 2007, 2015 by Tyndale House Foundation. Used by permission of Tyndale House Publishers, Inc.

Unless otherwise noted, all Scripture quotations are from the King James Version Bible (KJV) -Public Domain

Author's Contact
For speaking engagements:
Kebrina T. Robinson
www.kebrinarobinson.com
Paperback ISBN: 978-1-7345653-7-9
eBook ISBN: 978-1-7345653-8-6

CONTENTS

Dedication	3
Introduction	7
Chapter 1. The Age of Accountability	11
Chapter 2. Steps to Salvation	17
Chapter 3. Teaching Your Child to Pray	25
Chapter 4. Raising Children to Be Evangelists	33
Chapter 5. Be Careful Little Eyes and Ears	39
Chapter 6. 5 Powerful Prayers to Pray Over Your Child	47
Chapter 7. Parents' Prophecies	55
Chapter 8. Be Encouraged	67

INTRODUCTION

"I love them that love me, and those that seek me early shall find me."
Proverbs 8:17

As Christian parents, our primary goal should be to raise the next generation to serve Christ.

Easier said than done, right?

The goal becomes clearer when you consider the options. The reality is either you will raise your child to follow Christ or raise them to follow the world.

As I wrote this book, the Holy Spirit impressed Proverbs 8:17 strongly on my heart. The Lord says, "I love them that love me; and those that seek me early shall find me." The first part of Proverbs 8:17 speaks of mutual love between God and humankind. God's nature is always to love us unconditionally; however, for this love to be reciprocated, humans must be taught how to love God. The latter portion of verse 17 says, "those who seek Me early shall find Me."

"Early" in Hebrew is "*shachar*," which presents one as "earnest or diligent" in pursuit of understanding the Word of God. No matter how young your child is, every person is created to have a personal relationship with Jesus Christ; that is why God made the process of Salvation simple enough that children can understand and accept it.

Parents are pastors of the home, and it is through your teachings and examples that your children will learn to obey God, believe in His Word, and accept His gift of Salvation. Research shows that approximately fifty percent of teens who received Salvation were led to Christ by their parents (Barna Research Group, 2004). Other studies discovered that children in Christian homes usually accept Christ earlier in life than children in non-Christian homes, and the reason is apparent.

I want you to imagine that someone has given you an acre of land. You spend time tilling and preparing the soil, and then you leave without planting anything. After a while, you will discover that weeds have overtaken your once beautiful land. Now, think of your child as that beautiful acre of land. Would you let weeds and outside influences overtake your child? I am confident you answered with an absolute NO! Parents have the advantage that our young children believe everything we say. They will accept the reality of Jesus Christ in the same way they believe the Easter Bunny lie. Our greatest mistake is not sowing the right seeds at the right time. The home should be our first ministry and church, and it is where the seed of the Word of God can bear much fruit in our children's hearts.

Raising our children in the fear of the Lord is one of the most extraordinary responsibilities God has given us. The Bible gives several examples of parents who positively influenced their children's spiritual upbringing. For instance, in Genesis 18:19, the Lord highlighted why He chose Abraham to be "the Father of many nations" when He stated, "For I have chosen him so that he will direct his children and his household after him to keep the way of the LORD by doing what is right and just." Other exemplary guardians were Timothy's grandmother Lois and mother, Eunice. Their pious influence in his life was evident; the apostle Paul credited their godly influence in teaching the Scriptures to Timothy as the groundwork of his sincere faith.

It is God's will that our children learn the Scriptures from their earliest days. Timothy's experience was no accident. His grandmother and mother ensured that he gained a thorough knowledge of God's Word, and I implore you to do the same with your children.

Like Abraham, Lois, and Eunice, God has chosen you to lead your child to Him. For this reason, He gave numerous biblical instructions and models so you can take personal responsibility for your children's spiritual beginning. When Manoah, Samson's father, and his wife discovered they were going to be parents and that their son, whom God was giving them, had been chosen to be His great servant, they made the best decision. They went to God and said, "O Lord, please let the man of God whom you sent come again to us and teach us what we are to do with the child who will be born." And God listened to the voice of Manoah (Judges 13:8–9).

God listened!

What an astounding statement!

Are you ready to ask God for instructions on how to win your child to Him? God Almighty stooped to listen to Manoah, and He is waiting to hear from you.

Today, I encourage you to open your heart and listen to the direction the Lord has for you. In this book, we will explore several topics and questions that will help you along the way. I recommend you take notes and personalize every chapter, prayer point, and declaration to accomplish the task at hand. Take time to acknowledge God every time you pick up this book, and He will bless you with divine wisdom, knowledge, and understanding.

God bless you as you read!

CHAPTER 1

THE AGE OF ACCOUNTABILITY

In Christianity, the concept of the age of accountability is that there is a certain age at which children become accountable by God for their sins. For this reason, many people associate the age of accountability with death and judgment. But what if we were to view it from the standpoint of life and how we can introduce our kids to Jesus?

A few years ago, I had a conversation with a friend about the role of Christianity in his household. Even though he grew up in a Christian home and attended Christian schools, he was not open to talking to his son about Jesus. "I want Michael to decide for himself if he wants to follow Christ or not, so until he reaches the age to decide, I will not mention anything about Christianity to him."

He ended his point by saying, "He is just six years old. He is innocent!"

While allowing his young son to decide whether he wants to follow Christ, he unknowingly left the door open for Michael to be influenced by the world. Like my friend, folks may argue that young children are innocent, which is true to some extent. While his son may not have committed any personal sin, as descendants of Adam, we were all born in sin with sinful natures.

So, what is the exact age of accountability? According to Jewish customs, children become accountable at the beginning of their teen years when they celebrate their bar/bat mitzvah. Others believe the appropriate age is 20 years old, based on Numbers 32:11, which states: "Surely none of the men that came up out of Egypt, from twenty years old and upward, shall see the land which I swore unto Abraham, unto Isaac, and unto Jacob; because they have not wholly followed me." Nevertheless, nowhere in the Bible is a particular age of accountability mentioned. This led me to believe that accountability depends on God's grace and varies from person to person.

Almost thirty years ago, when I was just eight years old, I had a dream where I was falling into a bottomless pit of fire. At that time, I did not know about heaven or hell. I woke up in a panic and ran to my grandmother in the kitchen. After explaining my dream to her, she gently looked at me and said, "It's time to accept Jesus as your Savior."

To this day, I am grateful for the wisdom of my grandmother. From what I had explained, she knew I needed Salvation, and without inciting fear, she led me to Christ.

Not every child will have an experience like mine, but as Christian parents, we can be proactive like my grandmother and steer our kids in the right direction. From a young age, we teach our children right from wrong, and as their understanding increases, the difference between being good and bad also develops. When we introduce them to Jesus and discuss the price He paid for us, their understanding will increase further and grow into an awareness that sin displeases God.

One thing that I love about the Word of God is that it provides us with solutions for every issue in our lives. On the concept of right and wrong, the Bible says, in Proverbs 20:11, "The character of even a child can be known by the way he acts—whether what he does is pure and right." This verse tells us that, deep down inside, even at a young age, we all have a moral compass directing our thoughts and actions.

So how can we tilt the needle toward the right side? The answer is in Proverbs 22:6, where God instructed us to "Train up a child in the way he should go, and when he is old, he will not depart from it." Although children may not fully comprehend what it means to follow the Lord, they still need to hear the Gospel. Our children need to know that God loves them and that He sent His only son to earth to take away their sins.

Throughout the Bible, the responsibility God placed in the hands of parents is clear. None is more evident than Deuteronomy 6:6–7: "These commandments that I give you today are to be on your hearts. Impress them on your children. Talk about them when you sit at home and when you walk along the road, when you lie down and when you get up."

Regardless of how young our children are, as parents, we are responsible for teaching them about God. The world may say that they are too young and that we are forcing Christianity on them, but the world's opinion does not matter! Romans 12:2 tells us: "Do not be conformed to this world, but be transformed by the renewal of your mind." This mandate was for adults and children. As mentioned before, we are all descendants of Adam, born in sin with a sinful nature. Therefore, our children's minds must also be renewed.

The formative years of our children's lives are crucial. During this time, they develop their views on life and the world. A study conducted by the Barna Group, an evangelical Christian polling firm, found that nearly half of all Americans who accept Jesus Christ as their Savior do so before turning 13 (43%) and that two out of three born-again Christians (64%) committed to Christ before turning 18 (accessed April 22, 2019). For us, Christian parents, this is great and encouraging news. In these early years, we have the most influence on their physical, mental, and spiritual development.

As a special-needs child's parent, I would be negligent if I did not include these precious children in this discussion. While the scriptures do not openly state that children, including babies, who cannot choose to follow Christ will make it to heaven, there is no reason to believe that God would not mercifully save them. That said, we should not let cognitive disabilities keep us from acknowledging their need for a Savior. There are many reasons for not presuming too much about their disabilities. First, if we overemphasize their limitations, we can hinder their healing because we focus on their disabilities and not on the Healer. Second, even though someone is classified as nonverbal, it does not mean that the Gospel is not resonating in their mind and spirit. In this respect, if we believe that God is powerful enough to enter places we cannot see or understand, we should continue preaching the Gospel to our children, whether they "get" it or not.

I hope this new perspective on age accountability brings you insights and encouragement. Ultimately, everyone must decide to follow Christ on their own, but as loving parents, we can surely shepherd our children's hearts toward salvation. The quip, *"Do your best and let God do the rest,"* has always been my approach to helping my son live for Christ. We are all humans, and we will make mistakes, but it is imperative to be transparent in our Christian walk for our children's benefit. Pray with them. Talk to them about God. Share testimonies with them. Take them to church. Explore the Bible with them. Spend time worshipping together. And when you have done all you can, stand!

PRAYERS & REFLECTIONS

CHAPTER 2

STEPS TO SALVATION

> *"Peter replied, 'Each of you must repent of your sins and turn to God and be baptized in the name of Jesus Christ for the forgiveness of your sins. Then you will receive the gift of the Holy Spirit. This promise is to you, to your children, and to those far away—all who have been called by the Lord our God.'"*
> **Acts 2:38–39 NLT**

Here we find Peter preaching on the day of Pentecost, announcing to the attendees that Salvation's promise was not only for them but also for their children and their children's children.

That promise is still relevant today, and it applies to you as well. God is interested in saving your children only if you will allow Him to do so.

In the previous chapter, we addressed the age of accountability and why it is essential to talk to our children about God early. This chapter will discuss how we can encourage them to take the next best step: receiving Salvation.

Receiving Christ is a big decision, and understandably, you may have some concerns about lacking the training to lead your child. Still, God has given you the most important and influential role when it comes to influencing your child's path to Salvation. At this young age, your child is like a sponge ready to soak up Jesus' love, and as you live out your faith daily, leading your child to Christ will be organic.

Before we dive into the prayer of Salvation, we must address the first and most crucial step to take before speaking to our children: praying for them. Spending time in prayer and asking the Holy Spirit to prepare their hearts and minds will help increase their reception to the Gospel. Praying will also help you get the message across clearly and with confidence.

As you prepare to pray for your children, consider inviting your spouse or a friend from church to join you. Matthew 18:20 says, "For where two or three are gathered together in my name, there am I in the midst of them." Therefore, it is always good when a fellow Christian stands in agreement with you in prayer. You may need to pray numerous times in some cases, so allow the Holy Spirit to guide you. Here is an example of the prayer I used before speaking to my son about Salvation.

Dear Jesus, you promised to save me and my household, so I ask that You move upon _____'s heart to accept you as (his/her) Lord and Savior. Reveal yourself to my child and give (him/her) a heart to know you personally. Draw (him/her) close to you so that (he/she) may receive forgiveness and Salvation. Holy Spirit show me how to minister to my child; give me wisdom and the right words to say. I thank you for answering my prayers in Jesus' name. Amen.

Now that we have set the foundation, it is wise to prepare for questions that will most likely come up.

Here are the top three questions.

What Is Sin?

Sin is a defiance of the rules God established for humankind. Man's original sin was Adam's disobedience to God. Tempted and tricked by Lucifer, Adam and Eve disobeyed God and ate from the Tree of the Knowledge of Good and Evil. Since then, sin has been passed down to every person.

Younger kids may not fully understand the concept of sin, but they must be made aware that God has a particular way He wants us to live. You can explain to them that sin occurs when we choose to do things our way instead of God's way. A great way to teach the meaning of sin is to give examples of when someone disobeyed or took something that was not theirs. Teach these principles carefully because young children can feel that they are no longer saved once they have sinned.

Even though sin can be uncomfortable to discuss with your child, it provides the best opportunity to share the Gospel. Use this opening to explain that Jesus died to save us from our sins so that one day we can live with Him in heaven forever.

What is Salvation?

Salvation is simple but profound. In its rawest form, Salvation is the process of being saved from the power of sin and its consequences. It is a gift from God that comes through the sacrificial death and resurrection of Jesus Christ. The Bible says in Ephesians 2:8-9, "For by grace you are saved through faith, and this not of yourselves; it is the gift of God." In other words, we do not earn Salvation through our efforts but through personal faith in Jesus Christ as Lord.

For children, you can define Salvation as a special friendship with God. It is so special that He sent Jesus, His only son, to show us how much He loves us. Jesus came to Earth for the express purpose of God knowing humans personally, so He could protect, love, and teach them the right way to live a happy life.

Why is it necessary to receive Salvation?

In our normal human state, we are all sinners undeserving of heaven. Jesus' atoning death and resurrection have enabled us to partake in everlasting life; however, this privilege is guaranteed only to those who accept Him as their

Savior. Acts 4:12 clearly states, "Salvation is found in no one else, for there is no other name under heaven given to men by which we must be saved." Therefore, there is no Salvation apart from what Jesus freely gave us.

When discussing the need for Salvation with your children, be clear that it is the only way to have a relationship with God. Gently remind them how original sin separated man and God and how accepting Jesus closes that gap.

After you have prayed and prepared, using simple words that your child will understand, ask them to repeat this or a similar prayer.

Dear Jesus, I have not always done the right thing. Please forgive me. I believe You died and rose again to save me from my sins. I receive You as my Lord and Savior. Now, please help me to live for You the rest of my life. Amen.

Once your children have completed the salvation prayer, CELEBRATE THEM! Let them know that God is pleased with their decision to follow Christ and that everyone in heaven is holding a party in their honor.

A spiritual development plan is vital for your child's walk with Christ. This plan should include helping the child engage with the Bible and be a part of a Bible-believing church. From time to time, remind them of God's special promises, e.g., that He will never leave or abandon them (Hebrews 13:5). It is imperative to assure them that they are not on this journey alone and that you will follow up with teachings on the Word to help them grow and learn more about God. Share your excitement about Jesus with your child. Foster an environment that will encourage daily prayers, Bible reading, and evangelism.

Following Salvation, baptism is the next step in your child's spiritual journey. While the Bible teaches that baptism should occur after conversion, there is no biblical requirement that it must take place immediately. It is always crucial to make distinctions between baptism and Salvation. You can do so by explaining that the act of baptism does not save a person, but it is a public expression of becoming a Christian. Delaying baptism will not impact your child's Salvation, so if you are unsure whether your child is ready, I suggest that you wait. However, if they understand why they should be baptized and are prepared to proceed, they should proceed.

Finally, I would like to say a BIG congratulations. You just won your child to Jesus!

Steps to Salvation

PRAYERS & REFLECTIONS

CHAPTER 3

TEACHING YOUR CHILD TO PRAY

We all were designed to live in regular, ongoing fellowship with God. To build strong Christian practices in your children, you must teach them to pray as early as possible. By encouraging your children to pray, you are instilling the importance of prayer and helping them take advantage of the great privilege of communing with their creator.

For parents grappling with *"how young is too young to begin praying,"* you can use 1 Samuel 2:11 as a reference. The Scripture tells us that shortly after Samuel had been weaned (which traditionally took place between the ages of two and five), he "was ministering to the LORD in the presence of Eli, the priest." Although little Samuel, at that time, did not know the Lord personally, the child learned to minister by imitating the actions of the priest. In 1 Samuel 3:1-18, Eli helped Samuel learn to identify and respond to God's voice. The prayer that Eli taught Samuel, "Speak, Lord, for your servant is listening" (1 Samuel 3:9), allowed the child to receive a word from God that changed his life forever. Samuel's entire childhood reveals that God can and does operate powerfully in young children, but prayer and prayerful guardians are required.

Prayer expresses faith and trust in God. Through prayer, we find strength, guidance, wisdom, joy, and peace. Leading by example is often the best way to foster a healthy prayer life; however, some children may have difficulty thinking of who and what to pray about. To help spark some ideas, I have collated two methods to guide you and your child during prayer.

METHOD 1
The Hand Prayer for Younger Children

Visuals make a vast difference when teaching small children. The same is true for prayer. The hand prayer is a cute technique for teaching children to pray for others that is easy for them to remember. Have your kids draw and decorate their five finger prayer. Adding specific names or even drawings will make the prayer time fun and interesting.

THUMB — The thumb is the closest finger to the body. This finger will represent their close friends and family. Begin the prayer by spending a few minutes giving thanks to God for His protection over the child's parents, brothers, sisters, grandparents, aunts, uncles, friends, and classmates.

INDEX FINGER — The index finger is also known as the pointer. This prayer point is for leaders in their life or the people who point them in the right direction, like teachers, coaches, doctors, crossing guards at their schools, and pastors.

TALL FINGER — Use this finger to remind your child to pray for the people in authority, like the president, the military, and the police. Ask God to give them the wisdom to make the right decisions.

RING FINGER — Often called the weakest finger, it can be used to remember those who are sick, in trouble, impoverished, or suffering in some way. Pray that Jesus gives them strength, healing, and a new beginning.

LITTLE FINGER — The pinky finger is for their personal prayers. Tell your child that God wants to hear about their needs, especially when they put others first in prayer. Encourage them to pray for their physical and spiritual growth and ensure them that God is ready and able to supply all their needs.

Finally, when the hand prayer is complete, ask your child to join you in giving God a wave offering of gratitude and praise. The wave offering is a sign of victory that will help boost their confidence when approaching God; it assures them that He hears us if we ask anything according to His will (1 John 5:15).

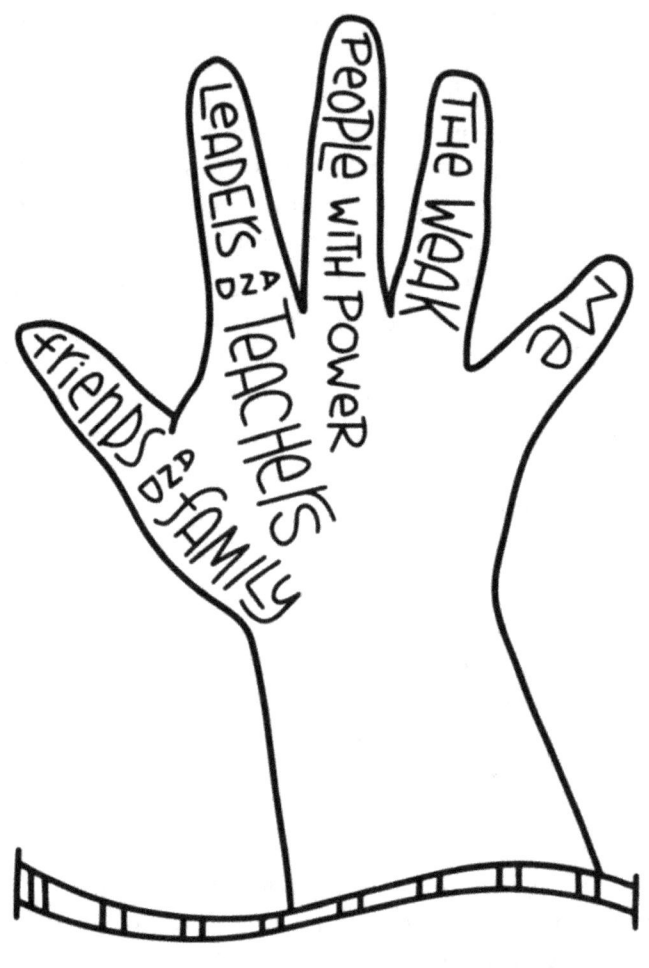

Image Source: Illustrated Ministry

METHOD 2
The Friendship Method for Older Children

For older children, the purpose of prayer should be presented as a tool for developing friendship with God rather than just getting something from Him. When the child sees prayer as relational instead of transactional, they will more likely share their innermost thoughts and feelings with Him. Here are some tips to help you get started.

INTRODUCTION — Describe prayer in words your children will understand. For example, you might start with something like, "Prayer is listening to and building a friendship with God."

LEARNING NAMES — Teach your children the many names of God, like Father, Friend, Shepherd, Provider, and Prince of Peace. Associating His names with His character will help build a picture of who God is and how much He cares about them.

SPENDING TIME — Praying using the Scriptures will help them understand how to hear from God through His word. The Scriptures will also provide solid proof that God does not change and that He can handle every situation.

TRUST BUILDING — Remind them that friendship with God is built on faith in Him and His wisdom; He knows what is best for us. This approach will teach them to trust Him even if things do not go their way.

Encourage your children to pray in the moment. Whether they are happy, sad, sick, or scared, God is there, waiting to have a dialogue with them—just like a best friend.

If you apply these tips when teaching your children about prayer, you can rest assured that your child will find a perfect friend. Friendship with God can be compared to one with a best friend—only better.

Through prayer and communication with God, they will learn that He is a friend who will never let them down, never betray their confidence, and always be with them in every situation.

Teaching Your Child to Pray

PRAYERS & REFLECTIONS

CHAPTER 4

RAISING CHILDREN TO BE EVANGELISTS

*"Go into all the world and preach the
Good News to everyone."*
Mark 16:15 NLT

In its purest form, evangelism is the direct outreach from Christians to unbelievers with the good news of God's saving grace. Evangelism involves calling people to repent, be born again, and follow Jesus Christ.

For centuries, powerful men and women of God have carried out this Great Commission through different channels like crusades, tract distribution, and door-to-door preaching, to name a few. The invention of radio and then television made it easier to reach the masses, even those living in obscure and hard-to-reach places.

Fast forward to the twenty-first century, and social media outreach has become the new frontline of evangelism. The increased usage of smartphones has changed how we communicate, inescapably shifting the way we talk to others about our faith.

Throughout the Bible, we read about great evangelists such as the Apostle Paul (Romans 1:15), Philip (Acts 21:8), and Timothy (2 Timothy 4:5). The Bible also mentions unconventional evangelists like the Samarian woman by the well who encouraged her neighbors to "come, see a man" in John 4:29 and the madman of the Gadarenes who returned home to tell his friends about his deliverance in Mark 5.

All of the aforementioned evangelists were great, but the most significant evangelist to ever walk this earth was Jesus Christ. The Bible says in Matthew 4:23 that Jesus went about proclaiming the gospel of the Kingdom. He also cured diseases and infirmities among the people. Jesus Christ is, was, and forever will be the *"Good News"* and our chief model for faith, obedience, prayer, good works, and evangelism.

When most folks think of evangelists, brave and gifted people like Billy Graham, Kathryn Kuhlman, and Benny Hinn come to mind. Rarely do we ever think of ourselves or our children as evangelists.

Apostle Paul, in the book of Ephesians, mentioned the office of the evangelist among the gifts that Christ gave to the church. This highly esteemed office is crucial for the church's growth, as it serves as a conduit between the unbeliever and the pastor.

By now, you are probably asking yourself: What does evangelism have to do with children? Well, although God has anointed special men and women for this office, all Christians possess the gift of an evangelist within them and are obligated to exercise it—and yes, that also includes our children.

Children, by nature, are natural evangelists. Whenever they hear or learn something new, their first instinct is to share it with their family and friends. This is the same when children decide to follow Christ; many are ready and willing to share Jesus with everyone they know. As parents, we need to remember that evangelism is not just an "adult thing." God can use our children's boldness and child-like faith to turn their friends' hearts toward Him.

In 2 Kings 5, the Bible tells us about a brave little girl who saved her master, Naaman, by evangelizing to his wife. Regardless of her situation, the little maid boasted about God and His prophet when she said to Naaman's wife, "If only my master would see the prophet who is in Samaria! He would cure him of his leprosy." She was confident in God's saving grace, and He honored her faith.

Where did such faith come from?

I am sure her parents and grandparents often shared their testimonies of God's goodness with her. They most likely took her along when they attended their religious ceremonies, and she must have listened as they spoke of God and His prophets. Her story proves that children who are exposed to God's love and power are capable of being soul winners.

Now that we have a more precise definition of evangelism, if I were to now ask you, "What kind of Christian does God use to spread the Gospel?"—I believe you would confidently add your children to the list. With that in mind, I formulated three simple but useful tips that can help you cultivate your child's natural desire to evangelize.

1. **Start Small** — As children begin to develop relationships in their neighborhoods and schools, encourage them to invite their friends to Sunday school. Bringing their friends to church is often the primary step in teaching children how to share their knowledge of Jesus. Your child may not be able to communicate the Gospel fully, but with their Sunday School teacher's help, they will be one step closer to winning their friends for the Kingdom.

2. **Be Consistent** — Apart from Sunday school, listening to gospel music and watching bible stories can also help saturate their hearts and minds with God's Word. It is a fact that faith comes by hearing, so regardless of which medium we use to teach our kids about Jesus, if they receive it, their faith will grow.

Praying with them every day and having them take turns praying out loud are great ways to make them feel comfortable with public speaking. Participating in ministry missions like food pantries and soup kitchens is also essential. By doing so, children will understand that evangelism is a lifestyle, not just something you do occasionally.

> 3. **Lead by Example** – Children learn most effectively through observation and imitation. When our kids see the joy we have in sharing the Gospel with others, they will often look for opportunities to imitate us. Adding simple phrases like "Jesus loves you" and "God bless you" to our salutations shows our children how even the smallest acts of kindness can help spread the Gospel. Take every opportunity to express to them that even though they are still young, they can help others understand God's love.

I urge you to see your children as valuable missionaries for Christ. Within them is a fearless tenacity that can be channeled into an invaluable soul-winning tool. Let us not underestimate our children's ability to help change their friends' lives for the better. Let us show them the way forward by introducing Christ to them early, being consistent in our actions, and leading by example. Our children will make great and powerful evangelists if we equip and encourage them to do so!

Winning your Child to Christ

PRAYERS & REFLECTIONS

CHAPTER 5

BE CAREFUL LITTLE EYES AND EARS

Like any new believer, your child will require guidance and nurturing to grow spiritually strong. In addition to reading the Bible and praying, we must limit outside influences that seek to contradict God's Word. Romans 12:2 states, "Do not conform to the pattern of this world but be transformed by the renewing of your mind." The word *"world"* refers to the *"world system"* or how non-Christians live their lives. 1 John 2:16 describes worldly living as "the lust of the flesh, the lust of the eyes, and the pride of life." By nature, human beings tend to chase worldly things in pursuit of joy and purpose, but as Christians, we have been instructed by God to transform our minds.

One way to help keep your children's minds protected from unhealthy, untrue, and distracting thoughts is to assist them in making wiser choices in videos, movies, music, and reading material. In His sermon on the mount, Jesus taught us that our eye is the soul's light, saying, "Your eye is like a lamp that provides light for your body. When your eye is healthy, your whole body is filled with light. 23 But when your eye is unhealthy, your whole body is filled with darkness. And if the light you think you have is actually darkness, how deep that darkness is!" Matthew 6:22-23 (NLT). He knew if we regularly watched the wrong things, we would likely pollute our minds with ungodly thoughts.

The Parable of the Sower in Matthew 13:1-23 taught us the human heart is like receptive soil; what we hear will determine what kind of soil our hearts will be. There are only two voices in the Spirit's realm—God's and the devil's. Although the media has tried hard to blur the difference between the two voices, one stark contrast is the emotions they invoke. For instance, a horror movie will fill your child's heart with fear, and before you know it, they will begin to experience anxiety and insomnia. On the other hand, godly shows will teach your child about moral truths and life lessons. In the end, their faith in Christ will grow, which is the goal for all new Christians.

The Bible says in Matthew 10:16, "Behold, I send you forth as sheep in the midst of wolves: be ye therefore wise as serpents, and harmless as doves." Thus, we must pay close attention to the subliminal messages the world is sending to our children. For example, if you skim through some popular cartoons, you will see that they are trying to make witchcraft a normal part of life. Right before our eyes, the networks are using bright colors and innocent-looking characters to make witchcraft appealing. Some even go as far as to create shows with so-called good witches. But is there any such thing as a good witch? The answer is an absolute "No!" According to Webster's dictionary, a witch uses destructive supernatural powers to influence or attract with allure or charm. So, if there are good witches, your next question should be, "By whose power?"

I think we all agree that music is omnipresent in our lives. Even if we are not playing it ourselves, it is in our cars, at the store, in the restaurant, and even at the doctor's office. We are never beyond its ubiquitous reach. Unfortunately for our children, much of the music and music videos in our society are ungodly. They present an incomplete picture of reality by omitting Christ while painting false images of relationships, sexuality, greed, and violence. Even in songs with no apparent negativity, you will hear notes of self-praise and narcissism if you listen between the lines.

As parents of young Christians, it is essential to be aware of the dangers of secular entertainment.

What are our children watching?

What are they reading?

What are their spiritual diets?

These are all questions we should take into consideration. As Christ-followers, we cannot afford to take the media's pervasive presence in our lives lightly. Although worldly media and activities can be enjoyable, educational, and uplifting at times, we should carefully evaluate what our children entertain and how these activities affect them.

Apostle Peter, in a letter to a group of new believers, states, "...So prepare your minds for action and exercise self-control. Put all your hope in the gracious Salvation that will come to you when Jesus Christ is revealed to the world. So, you must live as God's obedient children. Do not slip back into your old ways of living to satisfy your own desires. You didn't know any better then. But now you must be holy in everything you do, just as God who chose you is holy. For the Scriptures say, "You must be holy because I am holy" (1 Peter 1:13-16 NLT).

If we want our children to live the lives God has purposed for them, we must be diligent about guarding their media consumption. When talking to them about these hidden dangers, you can use the phrase "What would Jesus do?" as a guideline to only engage in activities Jesus would approve. The Bible reads in 1 John 2:6, "Whoever claims to live in him must walk as Jesus did." Therefore, using Jesus as a guide is a great way to help them evaluate what they let into their Spirit.

We cannot hide our children in bubbles, and there will be times when they will be exposed to worldly materials—for example, studying for a school project, watching the news, or reading about current events. When we begin to instill values and guidelines for making wise choices early, they will be more aware of Satan's devices and are more likely to guard their minds and hearts.

Choosing the right type of clothing is another way to protect your children's minds and spirits. Fashion is big business, and our children are bombarded with advertising daily. In recent years, we have seen noticeable changes, especially in girls' clothing. There is a growing trend of making adult clothing fit young girls, and although "mommy and me" styles look cute, our daughters are being made to grow up faster than they should. This trend can lead to the sexualization of our little girls, which can draw unwanted and unneeded attention.

Another trend that is being adopted by society is the obsession with skulls in children's clothing. Yes, skulls were a part of God's creation, but they usually symbolize death or darkness. For a long time, this morbid trend was associated with Halloween, but now it seems like every department has an overwhelming array of skull-themed clothing. Many parents think it is fashionable and harmless, but let me tell you: in today's world, everything has a meaning. It is either obvious or not so much. We are told in 1 John 1:5 "that God is light, and in him is no darkness at all." So it does not matter how cute or harmless the clothing may seem; there is nothing "cute" or "harmless" about darkness.

As I close, I encourage you to stay the course. When God saved our children, He called them to be different. What they watch on television matters. What they listen to matters, and what they wear matters. If we do not shun the little bits of darkness in our home, it can have lasting effects on our children. These subliminal messages from cultural influences can derail our children's walk with Christ.

Let us not give it any foothold in our household!

Evaluate what your child does for entertainment

- Would Jesus enjoy what my child enjoys? Yes/No
- Would Jesus find the same jokes funny? Yes/No
- Would Jesus read or watch the things my child does? Yes/No
- Would Jesus listen to the same music? Yes/No
- Would Jesus watch the same TV shows? Yes/No
- Would Jesus approve of my child's clothing? Yes/No
- What changes do you think Jesus would make to their entertainment choices?
- How much time do you think Jesus would want your child to spend on entertainment daily?

Be Careful Little Eyes and Ears

PRAYERS & REFLECTIONS

CHAPTER 6

5 POWERFUL PRAYERS TO PRAY OVER YOUR CHILD

Our children are precious gifts from God. Psalm 127:3–5 tells us that children are considered an inheritance and a reward. In the Bible, there are several accounts of people bringing their young ones to Jesus. Today, we can still take our children to Him, spiritually, through prayer.

Do not wait for a crisis to pray for your children. As Christians, we know prayer preserves, protects, and makes impossible situations possible; therefore, praying for our children is one of the best investments we can make as parents. Our prayers live before God, and our petitions allow us to bring Him our children's current and future needs.

In this chapter, you will find a collection of five special prayers to pray for your children to ensure that they receive that special touch from God.

1. PRAYER FOR PROTECTION

From Genesis to Revelation, the Bible assures us of God's protection. Sometimes God's protection comes in the form of peace and strength, and other times it comes physically, as in situations of averted accidents and dangers. As you pray, meditate on the fact that taking refuge in the shadow of His wing will bring security. (Psalm 57:1)

Dear Heavenly Father, I praise You that You are entirely in control of all things. Lord, I pray for Your emotional, physical, and spiritual protection over my children. I ask that You guard their minds and grant them discernment to make the right decisions. Give them a heart that trusts You and take away the desire to lean on their own understanding. Let them know that the only safe place is within You. Thank You in advance for Your protection, provision, and presence. In Jesus' name, Amen.

2. PRAYER FOR GOOD FRIENDSHIP

Proverbs 18:24 says, "A man with many friends can still be ruined, but a true friend sticks closer than a brother." That is why we need to pray for true friendship for our children. Though they are young, it is never too early to start praying.

Dear Jesus, I thank You for blessing me with parenthood. Lord, I bring my children's friendships before you. I know you did not intend for us to walk in solitude, so as iron sharpens iron, I pray You would lead Godly friends into my children's lives. Give them discernment to see situations from every perspective and integrity to treat others like they would want to be treated. Help them seek wisdom from others and grant them the ability to determine what advice they should listen to and follow. Finally, press upon their hearts that they have a friend in You. Assure them that You will never leave them nor forsake them even until their last day. I seal this prayer in Jesus' name. Amen.

3. PRAYER FOR THEIR EDUCATION

The Bible provides several excellent examples of scholars and academics. In Acts 7:20-22, we see that education helped Moses administer Israel's civil laws and codes. And remember Daniel, whose knowledge exceeded everyone in Nebuchadnezzar's kingdom. As we pray for our children, let us not forget that education works hand in hand with Godly wisdom. Let us pray:

Dear God, I thank you for the gift of education. As my child attends school, I ask that You impart Your Spirit of excellence and increase their desire to learn. I rebuke every spirit of fear, intimidation, violence, bullying, and perversion. I pray that You guard their hearts against the devil's schemes and preserve their minds from things that are not appropriate. Bless them with hearts of compassion for their fellow students. Put Your righteousness in their teachers' hearts and bless them as they create an environment where students can learn and flourish.

Father, as much as I want my child to thrive in their education, I want them to understand that fearing You and keeping Your commandments are the ultimate goals of their lives. Lastly, I ask that you give my child the courage to share Christ with their unsaved friends and teachers. In Jesus' Name. Amen.

4. PRAYER FOR GOOD HEALTH

God gave us our earthly bodies, and our health is of high importance to Him. The Bible says in 3 John 1:2, "I pray that you may prosper in all things and be in health, just as your soul prospers." Let us use this Scripture as a prayer point to intercede for our children's physical and spiritual health.

Dear Heavenly Father, thank You for the child who You have entrusted to me. Lord, I pray that You will shield and strengthen their body against diseases, sicknesses, and other health conditions. I come against every form of mental illness and ask that You bless their minds with soundness. Help them know that their body is the Holy Spirit's temple, and give them mindfulness that what they consume can harm or nourish them. I implore that You keep my child pure spiritually, emotionally, and physically. In Jesus' Matchless Name. Amen.

5. PRAYER FOR THEIR FUTURE SPOUSE

When we think about our little children, marriage is not the first thing that comes to mind. It may sound silly to pray for something that is so far into the future, but your child's future spouse will have a tremendous impact on their faith, happiness, and many important decisions in their lives. To ensure they make the most suitable choice, now is the best time to petition on their behalf.

Dear Jesus, I pray that you bless my child with the right spouse. As they grow up in their respective homes, let them live according to Your Will and Word so that they may enjoy a healthy marriage rooted in strong common faith. Guard their hearts and minds, and let purity reign in their lives. Lord, may they appreciate each other's virtue and gifts, and may they value each other's friendship. May they both possess humility and gentleness so that their lives together will be filled with love and laughter. Help them know that marriage is a serious but beautiful commitment and that every trying situation can be resolved with love, respect, and your Word. Until their paths cross, Father, keep them focused and reliant on You. Give their parents wisdom to raise an honorable child and grant me the same knowledge. Bless them as You promise us all, beyond what we can imagine or ask for. In Jesus' Name. Amen.

These five prayer points are just examples to guide you. I urge you to write additional, more personalized points that can address your child's specific needs. There is a battle over our children, and the enemy would love nothing more than to destroy them in their young years. He is wicked, deceitful, and cunning. When he cannot attack you, he will go after your children—Do not let him win!

Persistent prayer produces power, so do not let up or give in. When you pray, be specific, exercise your believer's authority, and hold on to the promises that God has for your child's life. You Are Already A Winner!

5 Powerful Prayers to Pray Over Your Child

PRAYERS & REFLECTIONS

CHAPTER 7

PARENTS' PROPHECIES

> *"In the beginning God created the heaven and the earth. And the earth was without form, and void; and darkness was upon the face of the deep. And the Spirit of God moved upon the face of the waters. And God said, let there be light:*
> *and there was light."*
> **Genesis 1:1–3**

God created the world by speaking it into existence, and we, as His children, have the same creative power inside us. The words that we speak can bless or curse, and what we say about ourselves and our children determines whether we are victorious or vanquished. God desires us to use our words to change situations that are not in line with His Word. We can achieve this by professing what God has declared already about us, our children, and our circumstances.

One of our greatest acts as Christian parents is committing our children and our childrearing to the Lord. It is essential to regularly soak our children in prayer—trusting, believing, and declaring His promises over them. The devil wants us to speak contradictory words of despair, doubt, and disappointment over our children, but he is powerless against us if we do not say words that agree with his plan. The enemy needs our words to gain authority in our lives, so we should never underestimate the importance of speaking blessing and truth over our children.

Prayer is our most potent weapon in protecting our children, even in places where we are not physically present. In the morning or throughout the day, call out your children's names as you declare the Word of God over their lives; inject their names into scriptures as you prophesy the word of God over them. Lay your hands on them when they are asleep and prophetically declare the word of God over them.

It is time to speak God's word with power! Are you ready to pray specific, powerful, promise-filled, hope-inspired prayers over your child? Are you ready to declare whom you want your child to be with God's help? If so, here are thirty scriptures and confessions to get you started as you begin standing on God's Word for your child.

Scripture Reference — "Be strong and courageous. Do not be afraid, do not be discouraged, for the Lord your God will be with you wherever you go." Joshua 1:9

Prophetic Declaration — My child is resilient and courageous. They will not be afraid or discouraged, for the Lord God is with them wherever they go.

Scripture Reference — "Do not let any unwholesome talk come out of your mouths, but only what is helpful for building others up according to their needs, that it may benefit those who listen." Ephesians 4:29

Prophetic Declaration — No unwholesome talk will come out of my child's mouth. He/She will only speak what helps build others up according to their needs, that it may benefit those who listen.

Scripture Reference — "Only fear the Lord and serve him faithfully with all your heart. For consider what great things he has done for you." 1 Sam. 12:24

Prophetic Declaration — My child will only fear the Lord and serve him faithfully with all their heart.

Scripture Reference — "For you bless the righteous, O Lord; you cover him with favor as with a shield." Psalm 5:12

Prophetic Declaration — Like a shield, the Lord's favor covers my child.

Scripture Reference — "Whoever walks with the wise becomes wise, but the companion of fools will suffer harm." Prov. 13:20

Prophetic Declaration — My child is wise, and they will not walk in the companion of fools to suffer harm.

Scripture Reference – "May the grace of the Lord Jesus Christ, and the love of God, and the fellowship of the Holy Spirit be with you all." 2 Corinthians 13:14

Prophetic Declaration – The grace of the Lord Jesus Christ, the love of God, and the Holy Spirit's fellowship will be with my child always.

Scripture Reference – "And you will know the truth, and the truth will set you free." John 8:32

Prophetic Declaration – My child knows the truth, and they are free.

Scripture Reference – "But those who hope in the Lord will renew their strength. They will soar on wings like eagles, they will run and not grow weary, they will walk and not be faint." Isaiah 40:31

Prophetic Declaration – My child will soar on wings like eagles. They will run and not grow weary, and they will walk and not be faint.

Scripture Reference – "Do nothing from rivalry or conceit, but in humility count others more significant than yourselves. Let each of you look not only to his own interests, but also to the interests of others." Philippians 2:3-4

Prophetic Declaration – My child is humble because they look not only to their interests but also to others' interests.

Scripture Reference – "...for the joy of the LORD is your strength." Nehemiah 8:10

Prophetic Declaration – The joy of the Lord is my child's strength.

Scripture Reference – "Children, obey your parents in the Lord, for this is right." Ephesians 6:1

Prophetic Declaration – My child will obey me in the Lord, for this is right.

Scripture Reference – "Know this, my beloved brothers: let every person be quick to hear, slow to speak, and slow to anger." James 1:19

Prophetic Declaration – My child is patient. He/she is quick to hear, slow to speak, and slow to anger.

Scripture Reference — "You keep him in perfect peace whose mind is stayed on you, because he trusts in you." Isaiah 26:3

Prophetic Declaration — My child is in perfect peace because his/her mind stays on God, and he/she trusts in Him only.

Scripture Reference — "And my God will supply every need of yours according to his riches in glory in Christ Jesus." Philippians 4:19

Prophetic Declaration — The Lord will supply all my child's needs according to his riches in glory in Christ Jesus.

Scripture Reference — "For I know the plans I have for you, declares the Lord, plans for welfare and not for evil, to give you hope and a future." Jeremiah 29:11

Prophetic Declaration — God has great plans for my child. These plans are for good and not for evil; they will give him/her hope and a bright future.

Scripture Reference — "The Lord will watch over your coming and going both now and forevermore." Psalm 121:8

Prophetic Declaration — My child is protected, for the Lord watches over their comings and goings.

Scripture Reference — "For God gave us a spirit not of fear but of power and love and self-control." 2 Timothy 1:7

Prophetic Declaration — *My child is well disciplined because God did not give him/her a spirit of fear but of power, love, and self-control.*

Scripture Reference — *"Be strong in the Lord and in his mighty power. Put on the full armor of God so that you can take your stand against the devil's schemes." Ephesians 6:10–11*

Prophetic Declaration — *My child has on God's full armor and will not fall for the devil's schemes.*

Scripture Reference — *"Trust in the LORD with all your heart and lean not on your own understanding; in all your ways submit to him, and he will make your paths straight." Proverbs 3:5–6*

Prophetic Declaration – *My child trusts in the Lord and does not lean on his/her own understanding.*

Scripture Reference – *"Ye are of God, little children, and have overcome them: because greater is he that is in you, than he that is in the world." 1 John 4:4*

Prophetic Declaration – *My child is victorious because greater is He that is in him/her than he that is in the world.*

Scripture Reference – *"Therefore, keep the words of this covenant and do them, that you may prosper in all that you do." Deuteronomy 29:9*

Prophetic Declaration – My children will walk in triumph in every situation and shall prosper in everything they do.

Scripture Reference – "Nay, in all these things, we are more than conquerors through him that loved us." Romans 8:37

Prophetic Declaration – Christ lives in my child, and he/she is more than a conqueror.

Scripture Reference – "Jesus said unto him, 'If thou canst believe, all things are possible to him that believeth.'" Mark 9:23

Prophetic Declaration – My child believes in God's Word, and he/she will ignore voices contrary to His Word.

Scripture Reference – "But upon mount Zion shall be deliverance, and there shall be holiness, and the house of Jacob shall possess their possessions." Obadiah 1:17

Prophetic Declaration – My children now possess their possessions, and all doors are open for them.

Scripture Reference – "Beloved, I pray that all may go well with you and that you may be in good health, as it goes well with your soul." 3 John 1:2

Prophetic Declaration – Sickness is not my child's portion, and he/she lives in divine health.

Scripture Reference – "And the Lord shall make thee the head, and not the tail, and thou shalt be above only, and thou shalt not be beneath; if that thou hearken unto the commandments of the Lord thy God, which I command thee this day, to observe and to do them." Deuteronomy 28:13

Prophetic Declaration – My child will be the head and never the tail, above always and never beneath.

Scripture Reference – "The eyes of your understanding being enlightened; that ye may know what is the hope of his calling." Ephesians 1:18

Prophetic Declaration – My child's eyes will be open to understanding the Lord's way. Their eyes will not lead them into sin, but Christ will enlighten them.

Scripture Reference – "And thine ears shall hear a word behind thee, saying, this is the way, walk ye in it, when ye turn to the right hand, and when ye turn to the left." Isaiah 30:21

Prophetic Declaration – My child will hear the Lord's word, and he/she will never depart from it, all the days of his/her life.

Scripture Reference – "I can do all things through Christ, which strengtheneth me." Philippians 4:13

Prophetic Declaration – My child can do all things through Christ, who strengthens him/her.

Scripture Reference – "A man's heart deviseth his way: but the Lord directeth his steps." Proverbs 16:9

Prophetic Declaration – My child's steps are ordered by God, and the Lord himself shall lead him/her.

Hallelujah!

Dear Heavenly Father, I agree with these parents and ask that You hide their children in Your secret place where no evil shall befall them and no harm will move near their dwelling. May Your Spirit of wisdom and understanding rest heavily upon their children so that they might grow in knowledge and fear of You. May they learn to delight themselves in You that they may flourish and be fruitful in everything they do. Lord, pour a divine blessing upon them and bless them everywhere they go. As Your goodness and mercy follow them all the days of their lives, may their parents reap the fruits of their labor and joyfully watch their children blossom into the people You created them to be. In Jesus' Name. Amen.

Parents' Prophecies

PRAYERS & REFLECTIONS

CHAPTER 8

BE ENCOURAGED

> *"And the Lord said unto Noah, Come thou and all thy house into the ark; for thee have I seen righteous before me in this generation."*
> **Genesis 7:1**

Our young children rely on us for direction in life in just about every way, and this makes the home one of the best places to raise disciples. In 2 Timothy 3:16, Paul tells Timothy that all Scripture is useful for training in righteousness, which means there is an abundance of guidance for parents in the Bible.

While I was preparing for this book, the Lord brought the story of Noah to my recollection.

"7 And the Lord said, I will destroy man whom I have created from the face of the earth; both man, and beast, and the creeping thing, and the fowls of

the air; for it repenteth me that I have made them. 8 But Noah found grace in the eyes of the Lord. 9 These are the generations of Noah: Noah was a just man and perfect in his generations, and Noah walked with God. 10 And Noah begot three sons, Shem, Ham, and Japheth. 11 The earth also was corrupt before God, and the earth was filled with violence. 12 And God looked upon the earth, and behold, it was corrupt; for all flesh had corrupted his way upon the earth. 13 And God said unto Noah: The end of all flesh is come before me; for the earth is filled with violence through them; and, behold, I will destroy them with the earth. 14 Make thee an ark of gopher wood; rooms shalt thou make in the ark, and shalt pitch it within and without with pitch. 15 And this is the fashion which thou shalt make it of: The length of the ark shall be three hundred cubits, the breadth of it fifty cubits, and the height of it thirty cubits. 16 A window shalt thou make to the ark, and in a cubit shalt thou finish it above; and the door of the ark shalt thou set in the side thereof; with lower, second, and third stories shalt thou make it. 17 And, behold, I, even I, do bring a flood of waters upon the earth, to destroy all flesh, wherein is the breath of life, from under heaven; and everything that is in the earth shall die. 18 But with thee will I establish my covenant; and thou shalt come into the ark, thou, and thy sons, and thy wife, and thy sons' wives with thee." Genesis 6:7–18

That Noah did not conform to the world's way of doing things stood out to me. He built an enormous boat in the middle of the desert, with no signs of rain or water. He made the ark by doing what God had commanded him to do. God showed him step-by-step how to build the ark, which was for the Salvation of both him and his whole family.

Noah was the pastor of his home, a true shepherd who convinced his wife and children to follow him on an endeavor when everyone around him thought it foolish. That decision led to their Salvation and that of the whole human race.

I am confident that after reading the passage, you will begin to see some similarities between you and Noah. Just as God provided Noah with instructions for building the ark, God has given you instructions for bringing Salvation to your children. Yes, Noah's children were adults, but they chose to follow their father's leadership because they were raised from childhood to obey their father and the Lord.

The Salvation of Noah's family says a lot about Noah, and the Bible provides vital insights into how he accomplished it.

First, Genesis 6:9 states, "Noah was a just man and perfect in his generations, and Noah walked with God." When you walk with God, you factor Him into your everyday life and your decision-making. You spend time praying and talking with Him throughout the day. Noah lived righteously, which enabled him to draw near to God and become a friend of God. Spending time with God should be paramount for all Christians, but it is even more important for parents seeking to win their children to the Lord.

Second, Noah heard the voice of God. If you go on a walk with your friend, what do you do during your walk? Besides the obvious (walking), you are having a conversation, sharing things on your mind, and listening to your friend's responses. When we draw near to God, He begins to speak to us, guiding and directing our steps to what we should do. God showed Noah precisely how to make the ark to save his family, and through His Word, He has also given us guidance to save ours.

Lastly, Noah was an obedient and faith-filled man. Hebrews 11:7 reveals, "It was by faith that Noah built a large boat to save his family from the flood. He obeyed God, who warned him about things that had never happened before. By his faith, Noah condemned the rest of the world, and he received the righteousness that comes by faith." When you put your faith in God, your relationship with Him takes center-stage in your life. When God is your focus, the outside voices saying your child is too young to follow Christ will become obsolete.

I am sure there were contradictory voices in Noah's time too, but did he listen? No! Otherwise, he would have failed his mission.

The world may come against you; it may laugh at you or disparage you for being different. It may even call you crazy or old-fashioned, but people laughed at Noah, too, right up until they all drowned.

Just remember that!

You are reading this book because the moment has come to win your child over to Christ. So, the question is, are you ready and willing to do what it takes to save your son or daughter? Noah labored hard to build the ark, and you will have to work hard also. It will cost you a lot to go against public opinion; however, it will cost you even more not to.

Today, I pray that you remain strong and diligent on this journey. The Bible says in Galatians 6:9, "And let us not be weary in well doing: for in due season, we shall reap, if we faint not." Focus on raising God-fearing children, and you will reap the reward of well-rounded Christian adults who will eventually be your grandchildren's parents – fulfilling the promise of Acts 2:39. As you continue to seek God's guidance, the Holy Spirit will equip you with patience, wisdom, and everything you need to win your child. Parenting is one of the most fulfilling experiences in life, and God has chosen you to do this most cherished work.

You got this!

Winning your Child to Christ

PRAYERS & REFLECTIONS

www.ingramcontent.com/pod-product-compliance
Lightning Source LLC
Chambersburg PA
CBHW071032080526
44587CB00015B/2584